# SHARKS

# LETTER TO PARENTS

Dear Parents,

*Sharks* is an engaging early reader for your child.
It combines simple words and sentences with stunning
images of sharks. Here are some of the many ways you
can help your child learn to read fluently.

## Before Reading
- Look at the book's cover together. Discuss the title and
the blurb on the back.
- Ask your child what he or she expects to find inside.
- Discuss what your child already knows about sharks.

## During Reading
Encourage your child to:
- Look at and explore the pictures.
- Sound out the letters in unknown words.
- Use the glossary to learn new words.

Ask questions to help your child engage more deeply with
the text. While it's important not to ask too many questions,
you can include a few simple ones, such as:
- Can you point to this shark's gills?
- Would you like to meet this shark? Why or why not?
- How do you think this shark got its name?